Savvy

Girls Rock

GIRLS REBEL!

Amazing Tales of Women who Broke the Mold

BY HEATHER E. SCHWARTZ

Consultant:
Julie Novkov
Professor of Political Science and
Women's Studies
University at Albany
State University of New York

CAPSTONE PRESS
a capstone imprint

Library of Congress Cataloging-in-Publication Data
Schwartz, Heather E.
 Girls rebel! : amazing tales of women who broke the mold / by Heather E. Schwartz.
 pages cm.—(Savvy. Girls rock!)
 Includes bibliographical references and index.
 Summary: "Through narrative stories, explores females who fought for their beliefs, broke society's rules, and forever changed the world"—Provided by publisher.
 Audience: Grade 4 to 6.
 ISBN 978-1-4765-0232-8 (library binding)—ISBN 978-1-4765-3562-3 (ebook pdf)
 1. Women—Biography—Juvenile literature. I. Title.
 CT3207.S39 2014
 920.72—dc23
 [B]   2013010927

Editorial Credits
Jennifer Besel, editor; Veronica Scott, designer; Wanda Winch, media researcher; Laura Manthe, production specialist

Photo Credits
Alean Bowser, 15; AP Images: Express Newspapers, 20, Kwesi Owusu, 19 (top), Musadeq Sadeq, 26, stf, 36; Capstone: Dave Hoover and Bill Anderson, 31 (back); Corbis: Bettmann, 49 (right), 54, Bureau L.A. Collection, 32, Lynn Goldsmith, 33 (t), Sygma/Andrew Lichtenstein, 28, Sygma/JP Laffont, 46; Courtesy of Clipart ETC, Florida Center for Instructional Technology, USF, 12 (r); Courtesy of New Jersey Office of the Governor, photo by Tim Larsen, 44; CriaImages.com: Jay Robert Nash Collection, 53 (t, b–l); Getty Images Inc: AFP/Cornelius Poppe, 18, FPG/Hulton Archive, 48, Tim Graham, 47, Time Life Pictures/Margaret Bourke-White, 51 (bottom); Karen Wong Photography, 27; Library of Congress: Prints and Photographs Division, 8 (t), 13 (t, b), 14, 24 (l, r), 30, 31, 38, 39, 41 (all), 42, 43, 49 (inset), 50 (all), 51 (t), 58, 59 (all), 60; NASA, 4, JSC/Robert Markowitz, 5; National Domestic Workers Alliance, 45; Newscom: dpa/picture-alliance/Stefan Scheuer, 19 (b), Everett Collection, 57, Getty Images Inc/AFP/Jens Kalaene, 22, Getty Images Inc/AFP/Jewel Samad, 21, KRT, 34, 55, M.G.M., 53 (r), MCT/Richard Sennott, 23, Richard B. Levine, 35, SIPA/Alfred, 7, Zuma Press/Nancy Kaszerman, 11, 17, Zuma Press/ Snap, 52; Shutterstock: Anna Paff, 64, Binkski, cover, 1 (background), Canicula, 12-13 (books), Cienpies Design, 10, Denis Barbulat, 12 (l), Dfree, 33 (b), Ensuper, 8-9 (airplane design), grynold, cover, 1 (woman, flag), Irina Nartova, 28-29 (back), Jakub Krechowicz, 58-59 (old book), Michael Rosskothen, 24-25 (back), Molodec, 52-53 (back), Natykach Nataliia, 32-33 (back), pashabo, 3, PhotoHouse, 58-59 (wood), Pokaz, 54-55 (back), R_lion_O, 62-63 (back), sniegirova mariia, 54-55 (postcard), Traudl, 41-43 (flag); SuperStock Inc: ClassicStock.com, 49 (l); U.S. Air Force, 8 (b), 9 (r); USAFA McDermott Library SMA 329, 9 (l)

Direct quotations are placed within quotation marks and appear on the following pages. Other pieces written in first-person point of view are works of creative nonfiction by the author.
p5: http://www.people.com/people/archive/article/0,,20085312,00.html; p7: http://www.progressive.org/mag_intv0904; p10: http://www.biography.com/people/temple-grandin-38062?page=1; p15: http://www.biography.com/people/ rosa-parks-9433715?page=2; p29: http://www.youtube.com/watch?v=RF2NlAJzBps&feature=related; p31: http://www. biography.com/people/harriet-tubman-9511430?page=1; p32: http://snltranscripts.jt.org/77/77nconeheads.phtml; p33: http://snltranscripts.jt.org/79/79nupdate.phtml; http://snltranscripts.jt.org/76/76qupdate.phtml; p40: http:// womenshistory.about.com/od/quotes/a/lucretia_mott.htm; http://womenshistory.about.com/cs/quotes/a/alice_paul.htm; http://www.classwarfareexists.com/signature-quotes-lucy-burns/#axzz29bVHt5wR; http://womenshistory.about.com/ library/qu/blquston.htm; p45: http://www.time.com/time/video/player/0,32068,1567605638001_2112245,00.html; p47: http://transcripts.cnn.com/TRANSCRIPTS/0711/22/siu.01.html; p52: http://www.brainyquote.com/quotes/ quotes/k/katharineh100041.html

Printed in the United States of America in North Mankato, Minnesota.
082014   008409R

REAL REBELS

Throughout history women have fought for what they believed in. They fought for the environment, animals, or other people. They pushed for protection under the law. They challenged society's rules for women.

They didn't give up, and they didn't back down.

Rebellious women have made powerful, lasting changes. They had the guts to stand up for their ideas. And they have made the world a better place.

Rebellious girls rock!

It was a sweltering afternoon in Texas in 1983. Reporters crowded together at the Johnson Space Center. They were eager to speak with astronaut Sally Ride.

SALLY RIDE

MAY 26, 1951–JULY 23, 2012

In just a few weeks, she would board the shuttle *Challenger* for a 147-hour space flight. And she would become the first American woman in space.

"Will the flight affect your reproductive organs?" one reporter asked. Ride tried to be polite. "There's no evidence of that," she replied.

"Do you weep when things go wrong on the job?" another inquired. "How come nobody ever asks Rick those questions?" Ride wondered aloud, referring to *Challenger* Captain Rick Hauck.

"Will you become a mother?" At that, Ride finally smiled. "You notice I'm not answering," she said.

The reporters' questions weren't the only examples of prejudice Ride faced. Talk show host Johnny Carson joked that the shuttle's launch would be postponed until she found a purse to match her shoes. But none of it phased Ride.

Athletic by nature, she was physically fit and in great condition. She'd earned a PhD in astrophysics. She was a member of the first class at NASA to include women. She'd competed against about 1,000 applicants for this chance.

And she was ready to make history.

On June 18, 1983, Ride launched into space. On the six-day mission, she helped deploy satellites. She also did experiments on medicines in space and tested the shuttle's remote arm. When she landed back on Earth on June 24, she really had made history.

EILEEN COLLINS

NOVEMBER 19, 1956–

Sixteen years after Ride's famous flight, astronaut Eileen Collins built on Ride's success. On July 23, 1999, Collins took control of the shuttle *Columbia*. She became the first American woman to command a space shuttle.

Shirin Ebadi

JUNE 21, 1947–

I thought the Islamic Revolution would bring us freedom. But Iran's leaders in the late 1970s didn't believe women should serve as judges. I was the first woman in the history of Iranian justice to serve as a judge. But then I was dismissed from my job.

I could have given up. Actually, for a while I did. I had to. But after 13 years of being shut up in my house and being jobless, I had to fight back.

In 1992 I set up my own legal practice. I've taken on major cases representing women and children who've been abused and murdered. I've written books and articles defending their rights. Some people in my country don't believe women and children deserve to have their rights protected. But I know they deserve to be treated with respect. I won't stop fighting until we get it.

For my efforts, I've been arrested and even threatened with death. But I was also awarded a Nobel Peace Prize.

"ANY PERSON WHO PURSUES HUMAN RIGHTS IN IRAN MUST LIVE WITH FEAR FROM BIRTH TO DEATH, BUT I HAVE LEARNED TO OVERCOME MY FEAR."

WOMEN OF FLIGHT

Amelia Earhart

JULY 24, 1897-ABOUT JANUARY 5, 1939

Earhart used her first plane to fly higher than any woman had before. In 1932 she became the first woman to fly solo across the Atlantic Ocean. And in 1935 she became the first person to fly solo from Hawaii to California. The records she set proved women could fly higher and faster than anyone thought possible.

Bessie Coleman

JANUARY 26, 1893-APRIL 30, 1926

Coleman was educated, intelligent, and banned from flight school in the United States. Coleman was black, and she was female. The schools in her own country wouldn't accept African-Americans or women. Not one to take no for an answer, Coleman applied to a French aviation school. In 1921 she became the first black woman in the world to earn her pilot's license.

Nancy Harkness Love
FEBRUARY 14, 1914–OCTOBER 22, 1976

Jacqueline Cochran
MAY 11, 1910–AUGUST 9, 1980

Near the start of World War II (1939–1945), Nancy Harkness Love and Jacqueline Cochran both had a great idea at the same time. Why not train women as pilots? If women could fly at home, it would free up more men for combat. In 1943 Love and Cochran created the Women's Airforce Service Pilots (WASP). The organization gave women their first chance to learn to fly American military planes. WASPs tested planes, brought new planes to military bases, and towed targets for training.

NANCY HARKNESS LOVE

JACQUELINE COCHRAN

TEMPLE GRANDIN

Not many people in the world think like Temple Grandin. Grandin is a well-known scientist who holds a master's and doctoral degree in animal science.

> "NATURE IS CRUEL, BUT WE DON'T HAVE TO BE."

She has worked tirelessly to understand how to improve conditions for animals at slaughterhouses. She has redesigned meat plants so life and death are more humane for the animals. She says she can understand what the animals need because she thinks like one.

Grandin has a unique way of understanding the world because she is autistic. Autism is a condition that makes it hard to communicate. People with autism have difficulty understanding social cues such as tone of voice or facial expressions. They prefer to be alone, and they often develop a favorite topic which they study constantly.

But Grandin has worked hard not just to overcome her obstacles but to become a leader in her field. She does what no one thought she could.

PROVING THEM WRONG

A few hundred years ago, some people believed women were too emotional to be scientists. The evidence, however, says otherwise.

Caroline Herschel

MARCH 16, 1750–JANUARY 9, 1848

As a young girl in the late 1700s, Caroline Herschel was expected to take care of a household when she grew up. For a long time that was her role, in her parents' home and later in her brother's. But then she began helping her brother with his work making telescopes.

When Herschel's brother gave her a telescope, she used it to earn a place in history. She was the first woman to discover a comet. She eventually discovered eight of them. At age 96, she was honored with the King of Prussia's Gold Medal of Science.

Mary Somerville

DECEMBER 26, 1780–NOVEMBER 29, 1872

Like most people in the late 1700s, Mary Somerville's family didn't believe a girl needed much education. Her aunt felt an interest in reading was unladylike. Her father worried she'd hurt herself studying too hard. But Somerville wouldn't stop. She kept on learning Latin, algebra, and other subjects considered off-limits to girls. She studied in private and had help from an uncle who believed in her.

Somerville later proved educating herself was worth the effort. One of her most famous books began as a translation. But instead of just changing the language, she made a difficult math book easy to understand. She also used her scientific knowledge to predict the existence of Neptune and Uranus.

Her family may not have recognized her genius. But Somerville pushed until the rest of the world did.

Marie Curie

NOVEMBER 7, 1867–JULY 4, 1934

Born in Poland, Marie Curie was banned from attending the University of Warsaw because she was female. Being Polish, she was also banned from certain science jobs by the Russians who ran her country.

But Curie didn't let any of that stop her. She scrimped and saved to study physics and math in France. After graduating Curie accomplished more than she ever dreamed. She discovered two new elements, polonium and radium. She also became the first woman to win a Nobel Prize and was the first scientist to win two Nobel Prizes.

ROSA PARKS

FEBRUARY 4, 1913–OCTOBER 24, 2005

Barbara Walters

SEPTEMBER 25, 1929–

Women rebel for change throughout the world.
Their courage, strength, and passion inspire us all.

TAWAKKOL KARMAN
FEBRUARY 4, 1979-

Tawakkol Karman wants human rights abuses in Yemen reported and stopped. She organizes protests and founded Women Journalists Without Chains to help female reporters assist in the fight for human rights. The result: In 2012 a revolution ousted Yemen's corrupt dictator of more than 30 years.

LEYMAH GBOWEE
1972-

In 2001 there was no end in sight to Liberia's Second Civil War. Gbowee felt it was up to her to bring peace. She organized nonviolent protests that forced leaders to talk and come up with some answers. The result: The civil war ended in 2003.

ELLEN JOHNSON SIRLEAF
OCTOBER 29, 1938-

After Liberia's Second Civil War ended, a democratic election was held in 2005. Ellen Johnson Sirleaf was a popular candidate among women voters. She was known as the "Iron Lady of Africa" for showing determination during her more than 30-year political career. When she won, she became the first woman elected to lead an African nation. The result: Sirleaf helped heal a war-torn country by rebuilding schools and hospitals and working to restore the economy.

COMFORT FREEMAN

In 2002 Comfort Freeman joined forces with Leymah Gbowee to help found the Women in Peacebuilding Network (WIPNET). Their goal was to recognize women as peacekeepers. The WIPNET helped create the Women of Liberia Mass Action for Peace Campaign, which got women directly involved in confronting rebel leaders. The result: Peace talks moved forward until peace was achieved. And a female president was eventually elected in Liberia.

FREEMAN HELPED COORDINATE DEMONSTRATIONS FOR PEACE LIKE THIS ONE HELD IN A REFUGEE CAMP IN 2003.

ASMAA MAHFOUZ
FEBRUARY 1, 1985–

Mahfouz was already a founding member of the April 6 Youth Movement that used Facebook to call for protests in 2008. Three years later, she took another bold step. She posted an online video that showed her face. She declared her plan to publicly protest dictator Hosni Mubarak's rule of Egypt. She wasn't sure what would happen, but she didn't want to hide any longer. Her courage inspired both women and men. The result: Mahfouz sparked an uprising against the dictator.

The Taliban is a violent, radical group that took over Afghanistan and parts of Pakistan. The group had harsh ideas about where girls and women belonged in society.

The Taliban shut females out of schools, jobs, and hospitals. Durani and Yousafzai are two women who have risked their lives to fight back.

MALALA YOUSAFZAI
JULY 12, 1997–

When she was just 11 years old, Malala Yousafzai started blogging about her life in Pakistan under Taliban rule. She encouraged kids to speak up and defy the Taliban's rules. The world read her words. People listened as she told reporters that girls deserve an education and the right to play and sing. The Taliban listened too. In 2012 Taliban soldiers shot Yousafzai in the head. She survived, and the news of the attack spread her message even further.

TIMELINE

1996

The Taliban takes over Afghanistan.

1997

Women are banned from working in public.
Women and girls are not allowed to attend public schools.
Male doctors are forbidden to treat female patients who do not have a male relative with them.

1998

Private schools are banned from teaching girls older than age 8. Education is restricted to religious lessons.

2000

By 2000 hundreds of women are in prison for crimes such as laughing loudly, speaking to a man, or not following the dress code that requires covering their entire body.

2001

The Taliban is officially overthrown, although it still controls parts of the country.

MARYAM DURANI

1985–

If Maryam Durani would just keep quiet, she could stay safe. Instead, she's chosen to speak out for women's rights in Afghanistan—even though she knows Taliban leaders are listening.

As the owner of a radio station, Durani broadcasts her opinions for all to hear. She encourages women and girls to be confident and believe in themselves. She speaks against forced marriages and other traditions that violate women's rights.

For her work, she's been threatened, attacked, and seriously injured. Not everyone in her country believes women's rights are worth fighting for. But the dangers Durani encounters every day are not enough to make her quit.

In 2012 Durani won an International Women of Courage Award. Her enemies remain a threat, but the world recognizes her bravery.

Afghanistan's new constitution states that all citizens have the right to free public education. Taliban forces fight back. They attack government buildings, aid workers, and U.S. troops helping the new government.

Taliban forces grow stronger and launch major attacks.

Five former Taliban leaders are appointed to positions in Afghanistan's new government. The hope is that they can help keep the peace between the Taliban and the new leaders.

2002 **2003** **2004** **2005** **2007** **2010**

The new Afghan government puts $10 million toward improving women's employment opportunities. 1.5 million children return to school.

Afghanistan's new government declares men and women are equal.

The United Nations reports human rights violations against women continue, including forced marriages, random imprisonment, and torture.

Erin Brockovich

JUNE 22, 1960–

Erin Brockovich was working as a file clerk in a law firm when she discovered some very interesting files. The files told the story of a small town that had been poisoned by a large company's toxic waste. People living in the town had become sick and some even died as a result. But no one had ever held the company accountable.

Brockovich launched her own investigation. She gathered stories from townspeople about their health. Her work developed into a major lawsuit. In 2006 the legal battle won $333 million for more than 600 residents of Hinkley, California. And the company was ordered to clean up its mess.

Lois Jenson

Lois Jenson was a single mother earning low pay. When she took a new job at Eveleth Mines in northern Minnesota in 1975, she was pleased to earn a better salary. But she was one of only four women employed there. Her working conditions were terrible. Men at the mine swore at the female workers and verbally abused them. The men threatened physical violence. They even stalked the women when they weren't at work.

The women were too scared to do anything about the abuse. But then Jenson was attacked by a supervisor. Enough was enough. She finally filed a complaint with the Minnesota Department of Human Rights. Her actions started a legal battle that eventually won $3.5 million for a group of female workers. But more importantly, the case made companies take responsibility for and stop sexual harassment in the workplace.

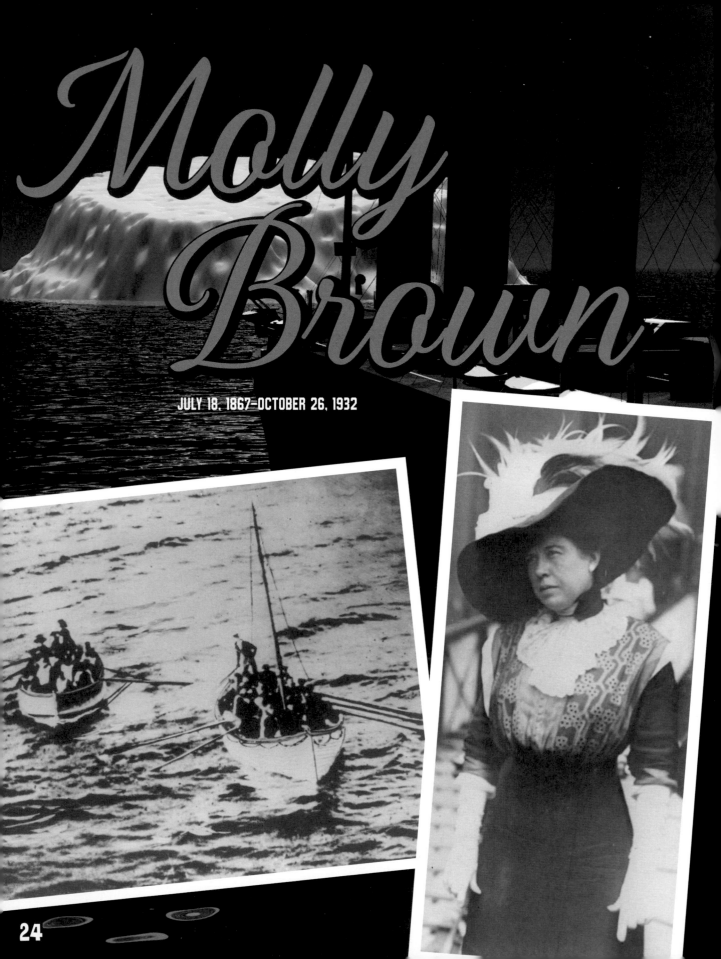

Molly Brown

JULY 18, 1867–OCTOBER 26, 1932

REPORTER: On April 15, 1912, the "unsinkable" ship *Titanic* went down, killing about 1,500 passengers. There might have been more victims if it weren't for Molly Brown, a passenger whose unusual bravery saved lives.

I'm here with Molly Brown. Tell us, Mrs. Brown, what did you do after the *Titanic* hit the iceberg? Did you rush to leave on a lifeboat, like many first-class passengers?

BROWN: No, I focused on loading others onto the lifeboats. I speak French, German, and Russian, so I was able to help many people who didn't speak English. Eventually, I did board a lifeboat myself.

REPORTER: What happened aboard the lifeboat you were on?

BROWN: Well, we passengers had to row to safety, you know. It wasn't very ladylike, I'm afraid. But I knew we were in an emergency situation. I rowed, and I told the other ladies aboard that they ought to row too.

REPORTER: What happened next?

BROWN: We saw the *Titanic* go down, and I was in a panic. We could hear people screaming as they tried to stay above water. I screamed that we had to go back and save more passengers. The quartermaster in charge of our boat said no. He thought if we put any more people on our lifeboat, we'd sink too. I tried to turn us around myself, but other passengers held me back.

REPORTER: The *Carpathia* arrived later, after hearing the *Titanic's* distress signals. What was the situation aboard the rescue ship?

BROWN: The survivors were devastated by the tragedy. I tried to nurse them and stay positive to improve their spirits. As we sailed for New York, I went around asking some of the wealthier passengers for donations. I felt it was our duty to help the poorer folks. We managed to raise more than $10,000.

REPORTER: Your heroic actions have made you famous. What will you do next?

BROWN: I don't really think I was a hero. I was just doing what needed to be done. I still want to help. I've founded the *Titanic* Survivors' Committee. We'll provide aid to families and build a memorial to commemorate this tragedy.

SADAF RAHIMI

1995–

When Sadaf Rahimi was growing up in Afghanistan, she saw a YouTube video of professional boxer Laila Ali. She was inspired and wanted to box too. But Afghan girls didn't become boxers. They didn't even play sports. The Taliban made the rules—and beat, beheaded, and shot those who disobeyed. Punishments were public events held in a former sports stadium.

Six years after the Taliban was overthrown, Rahimi began training as a boxer at that very stadium. She wanted to prove that girls could reach the highest level in boxing. She wanted to inspire other Afghan girls and let them know they could achieve anything they wanted.

It wasn't easy. The equipment at the gym was old and worn. She was teased and bullied for her choice of sport. Some of her coaches didn't even believe in her. But she kept at it.

Then in 2012 her hard work got noticed. Rahimi received a wildcard invitation to box at the 2012 Olympic Games. Wildcard invitations are given to countries that wouldn't otherwise have an athlete qualify. It's a chance for athletes to prove themselves and possibly compete.

In the end, Rahimi didn't get to compete. Her skills didn't match other competitors, and officials worried she'd get hurt. But she was a winner anyway. Rahimi proved hard work and perseverance could pay off. Her story was an inspiration to women everywhere.

RAZIA JAN

Razia Jan left Afghanistan in 1970 to live in the United States. When she visited her home country in 2002, she was horrified to see how the Taliban had changed Afghanistan. Even after the group was no longer in power, fathers didn't want to send their girls to school. Terrorists attacked female students by throwing acid in their faces and poisoning school water supplies.

Despite the dangers, Jan knew she had to open the Zabuli Education Center, near Kabul, Afghanistan.

She knew Afghan girls needed to learn. Without an education, they wouldn't be able to improve their lives.

Jan made sure the Zabuli Education Center would give girls that chance. She made sure the school was free to students. She built a stone wall around the building to protect them. She hired guards to test the water each day. They also check for poisonous gas inside the building.

By 2012, 354 girls were enrolled at the Zabuli Education Center. Some walk more than 45 minutes each way to school. Some are so excited they run. They want to become doctors, teachers, police officers, and engineers. Jan's efforts have given them a shot at a better future that was out of reach just a few years ago.

Julia Butterfly Hill

FEBRUARY 18, 1974–

Julia Butterfly Hill fell to her knees, put her head to the ground, and cried. She raised her head and then her hands.

"We did it!" she sobbed. "We did it!"

Hill had just climbed down from her tree house at the top of a 1,000-year-old redwood she called "Luna." She had spent 738 days in that tree. Without electricity. Without heat. Without a real bathroom.

A logging company wanted to chop down "Luna." Hill believed the tree was worth saving. So she climbed up the tree and swore to live there until it was saved. She got hundreds of letters from supporters. Friends used a pulley system to deliver them to her, and she answered every one.

When Hill started her "tree sit," she expected to live there for about a month. It took more than two years for her to reach an agreement with the logging company. The company finally agreed to let the tree stand and protect a 3-acre (1.2-hectare) area of trees around it as well.

Hiking barefoot after climbing down, Hill skipped and smiled. "It feels so good to be alive on this earth," she said.

She had every right to feel triumphant. At 25 years old, she had demonstrated to the world what personal commitment could do for the environment. She had saved "Luna." She had won.

Coretta Scott King

APRIL 27, 1927–JANUARY 30, 2006

She could have been overshadowed by her famous husband. After all, the Reverend Dr. Martin Luther King Jr. was the leader of the Civil Rights Movement. But Coretta Scott King made her own mark as a leader and an activist.

King organized Freedom Concerts featuring poetry, singing, and lectures. The concerts spread the message of the Civil Rights Movement and raised money for the cause. She took part in the Montgomery Bus Boycott and helped pass the 1964 Civil Rights Act.

King was dedicated to the work she did by her husband's side. When he was assassinated in 1968, she continued speaking out for racial equality. As a grieving widow, she founded the Martin Luther King Jr. Center for Nonviolent Social Change in Atlanta. She fought to make Martin Luther King Jr. Day a national holiday. King stepped up and is now recognized as a leader in the fight for social justice.

MARTIN LUTHER KING, JR.

Living The Dream

Let Freedom Ring

FEDERAL HOLIDAY COMMISSION

Harriet Tubman

ABOUT 1820–MARCH 10, 1913

"I WAS THE CONDUCTOR OF THE UNDERGROUND RAILROAD FOR EIGHT YEARS, AND I CAN SAY WHAT MOST CONDUCTORS CAN'T SAY; I NEVER RAN MY TRAIN OFF THE TRACK AND I NEVER LOST A PASSENGER."

Long before Coretta Scott King, Harriet Tubman struggled for one basic right—freedom.

In the early 1800s, slavery was a vital part of the economy in the southern United States. Slaves were expected to follow their masters' orders. If they didn't, they risked severe punishments, such as whippings.

Harriet Tubman was born a slave. As an adult she escaped and fled to the North where she could hide. But instead of hiding, she decided to help other slaves.

Tubman made the dangerous journey back to the South over and over. She gathered slaves to start the journey North. Using the Underground Railroad, a system of safe houses, Tubman made 19 trips South without being caught. She helped more than 60 slaves gain their freedom.

Funny Ladies

It seems that women have fought against every misconception in the world—and won. Comedy is no exception. Even today some people still believe women can't be funny.

Tell that to the women who made *Saturday Night Live* the powerhouse funny machine it is today. These comediennes created hilarious characters no one could ever forget. And they showed the world that ladies can make you laugh.

Laraine Newman

AS A CONEHEAD

MARCH 2, 1952–

"Good night, parental units."

Gilda Radner

AS ROSEANNE ROSEANNADANNA

JUNE 28, 1946–MAY 20, 1989

Jane Curtin

AS "WEEKEND UPDATE" ANCHOR

SEPTEMBER 6, 1947–

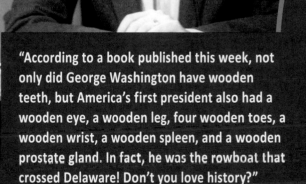

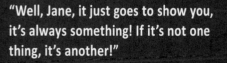

"Well, Jane, it just goes to show you, it's always something! If it's not one thing, it's another!"

"According to a book published this week, not only did George Washington have wooden teeth, but America's first president also had a wooden eye, a wooden leg, four wooden toes, a wooden wrist, a wooden spleen, and a wooden prostate gland. In fact, he was the rowboat that crossed Delaware! Don't you love history?"

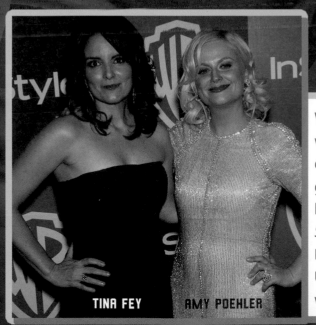

TINA FEY   AMY POEHLER

Without Curtin, Newman, and Radner, it would have been pretty tough for today's comediennes to get ahead. Thanks to their groundwork in funny business, Tina Fey became the first female head writer at *Saturday Night Live* in 1999. And when Amy Poehler joined her to coanchor "Weekend Update" in 2005, it was the first time two women had ever hosted the ongoing sketch.

Gloria

POOR
WORKING CONDITIONS
EXPOSED!

May 1963

Reporter Gloria Steinem is making headlines today. Steinem, working for *Show* magazine, went undercover in New York's infamous Playboy Club. There she discovered first-hand the problems women face in the workplace.

ACTIVIST
STARTS NEW
WOMEN'S
MAGAZINE

July 1972

Women's rights activist Gloria Steinem started a new magazine this month. The magazine is said to focus on politics and women's issues. *Ms.* magazine will cover controversial topics, such as domestic violence, which are not discussed in most other magazines for women.

Steinem

STEINEM PUBLISHES
FIRST BOOK

1983

Gloria Steinem's first book of essays came out this year. *Outrageous Acts and Everyday Rebellions* covers women's issues with wisdom and wit.

STEINEM WEDS
AT AGE 66

September 2000

Well-known women's rights activist Gloria Steinem married animal rights and environmental activist David Bale. The marriage shocked many, as Steinem was known for her disapproval of marriage. Steinem once again proved that she will do what she wants, no matter what anyone thinks.

BETTY FRIEDAN
FEBRUARY 4, 1921–FEBRUARY 4, 2006

Friedan was a leader in the women's rights movement in the 1960s. Her book, *The Feminine Mystique*, spread the message that a woman could have a satisfying life without being a wife or mother. That book kicked off the second major American women's movement for equal rights. Many educated women were housewives then. After reading the book, they started working in fulfilling careers outside their homes. Friedan became a leader in the movement she'd helped start.

ANGELOU

APRIL 4, 1928-

When Maya Angelou found her voice it was a voice of inspiration, understanding, and hope. But Angelou hadn't always had a voice.

When Angelou was a child her mother's boyfriend physically attacked her.

Her uncles took revenge and killed the man. But that didn't make Angelou feel better. In fact, she felt guilty for telling what had happened. The whole situation upset her so much she barely spoke for years. She had lost her voice.

Her teenage life didn't get much simpler. Angelou dropped out of school. She became a young, single mother. She worked as a waitress and cook to support her son. Her voice was lost in a world of stress and hardship.

Eventually ... slowly ... life got better. Angelou started dancing and singing. She started writing. She started protesting. Her voice grew stronger.

Then her voice boomed.

In 1970 Angelou released her memoir *I Know Why the Caged Bird Sings.* In the book she tackled violence, child abuse, family relationships, and prejudice. But it was her writing style that was truly unique. She made a true story read like fiction. She organized events by theme rather than the order in which they happened.

I Know Why the Caged Bird Sings was an international success. Angelou became famous for her writing. She used her voice to write more, including volumes of poetry that covered tough topics such as race, women's issues, and social justice.

Angelou didn't just find her voice. She let it sing.

MOTHER JONES

ABOUT 1830–NOVEMBER 30, 1930

She was one of the most dangerous women in America. Authorities didn't call her that because she carried a gun. Instead she was armed with intense passion that drew people to her.

Mary Harris Jones used her passion for good. She just wanted to take care of workers. In fact, that's how she got the name "Mother Jones."

In the late 1800s, laws didn't protect workers much. Workers in all types of jobs—coal miners, railroad workers, mill workers—could be forced to work long hours for little pay. They did dangerous work, and they got no help if they were hurt or sick. The workers formed unions to try to force employers to treat them better. But it was hard. Mother Jones worked tirelessly to help these union workers. She gave inspiring speeches and organized workers. With her help, labor laws began to change.

Mother Jones fought for workers' rights until the day she died. And she stood by them even in death. She asked to be buried in a place called Union Miners Cemetery.

GETTING THE VOTE

Women 100 years ago had to truly rebel to gain the most basic right in the United States—the right to vote. Many men didn't think women could be trusted to vote for leaders. They thought ...

WOMEN SHOULD BE THINKING ABOUT THEIR HOMES AND FAMILIES, NOT POLITICS.

WOMEN WERE TOO EMOTIONAL.

WOMEN WEREN'T SMART ENOUGH.

Thankfully, not everyone agreed with these views. And many were willing to fight against them. These women, called suffragists, toured the country, giving powerful speeches to sway public opinion. Many of these women did not live to see their fight succeed.

Lucretia Mott
JANUARY 3, 1793–NOVEMBER 11, 1880

"If our principles are right, why should we be cowards?"

Alice Paul
JANUARY 11, 1885–JULY 9, 1977

"There will never be a new world order until women are a part of it."

Lucy Burns
JULY 28, 1879–DECEMBER 22, 1966

"It is unthinkable that a national government which represents women should ignore the issue of the right of all women to political freedom."

Lucy Stone
AUGUST 13, 1818–OCTOBER 18, 1893

"'We, the people of the United States.' Which 'We, the people?' The women were not included."

Lucretia Mott

Alice Paul

Lucy Burns

Lucy Stone

Elizabeth Cady Stanton

NOVEMBER 12, 1815-OCTOBER 26, 1902

Elizabeth Cady Stanton was a powerful supporter of women's rights. She was an even more powerful leader. In July 1848 Stanton and other activists wrote the Declaration of Sentiments. Based on the U.S. Declaration of Independence, this document was an official call for female equality. Stanton insisted it include a demand for women's right to vote. Later Stanton helped form and lead organizations that worked tirelessly for women's rights.

Susan B. Anthony

FEBRUARY 15, 1820-MARCH 13, 1906

On November 5, 1872, Susan B. Anthony broke the law. She voted in the U.S. presidential election. By November 14, a warrant was out for her arrest. In a sense, it was a clear-cut case. She'd broken the law, so she went to trial and was convicted. The judge ordered her to pay a fine. But that wasn't the end of the matter. After the trial, many people saw Anthony as a hero. A woman had voted, reported at least one newspaper, and the country had survived. As for the fine, Anthony called it "unjust." In protest she refused to pay it—and she never did.

TIMELINE

1848

Lucretia Mott and Stanton hold the Seneca Falls Convention, the first of its kind for women's rights. It brought 300 men and women together to protest women's lack of rights and demand better treatment.

1866

Stanton and Anthony form the American Equal Rights Association, calling for the right to vote for black and white women and men.

1869

Stanton and Anthony form the National Woman Suffrage Association, an organization that worked to get the vote for women state by state.

ELIZABETH CADY STANTON (SEATED)
AND SUSAN B. ANTHONY

1872

Anthony illegally
casts a vote
in the U.S.
presidential
election.

1880

Mott
dies.

1893

Lucy Stone
dies.

1902

Stanton
dies.

1906

Anthony
dies.

1913

Alice Paul and Lucy
Burns found the
Congressional Union
for Woman Suffrage.

1920

The 19th Amendment
to the U.S. Constitution
grants women the right
to vote.

CAMI ANDERSON

1972–

At one alternative school, pregnant teens sewed pillows instead of learning math. At another, jailed teens were disrupted daily by people coming and going at all times. These students weren't getting a great education. They were misfits. Pregnant teens, drug addicts, criminals. No one cared about educating them because no one expected them to succeed.

No one except Cami Anderson. Anderson was superintendent of the New York City district in charge of these schools from 2006 to 2011. She believed these students could do better in school—and in life—if they had the right kind of help.

Critics said it wasn't worth the work to help these troubled teens. They said they wouldn't be able to get out of the situations they were born in.

But Anderson revamped the district. She weeded out weak teachers. She reorganized programs and closed failing schools. Soon, pregnant teens were in classes with regular students. Jailed teens got entirely new programs. Her changes increased student achievement, graduation numbers, and GED completion rates.

She proved that kids, no matter their situation, can achieve success. And she proved to the world that these kids are worth the work.

AI-JEN POO

FEBRUARY 5, 1974–

Many laws protected U.S. workers from unfair labor practices by the 1980s. But nannies, housekeepers, and caregivers to the elderly weren't covered by these laws. They could be required to work endless hours. Sometimes employers didn't pay them at all. Many of these workers didn't speak English. It was easy for abusive employers to take advantage.

Ai-jen Poo knew the jobs these domestic workers did was important and necessary. She couldn't stand by while they were treated so unfairly. So she decided to stand up for them. In the 1990s, she started organizing domestic workers. She cofounded Domestic Workers United.

She also helped form the National Domestic Workers Alliance to bring workers together. She worked to create New York's Domestic Workers Bill of Rights. In 2010 the bill became the first set of state laws to protect domestic workers from abuse on the job.

"Ever since I was little, I was really influenced by my mother and my grandmother, both of whom are very strong women who really valued all kinds of work including the work that it takes to raise families. But that work wasn't valued by other people, and so my mother always struggled. And I realized that so much of the unfinished business of the women's movement is really about bringing respect and dignity to this work."

AI-JEN POO

Mother Teresa

AUGUST 26, 1910–SEPTEMBER 5, 1997

The streets of Calcutta, India, were clogged with poor people desperate for help. Yet no one would go near them. These people belonged to a social class called the "untouchables." Getting involved to help them was considered unhealthy, not to mention a waste of time.

Mother Teresa, a nun in a Calcutta school, had a different opinion. In 1948 she felt called by God to do something drastic. She left her convent to start her own order of nuns. They offered food, shelter, medicine, and love to people cast out by society.

By touching the untouchables, Mother Teresa inspired others to do the same. Her mission to help the poorest of the poor spread throughout the world.

Princess Diana

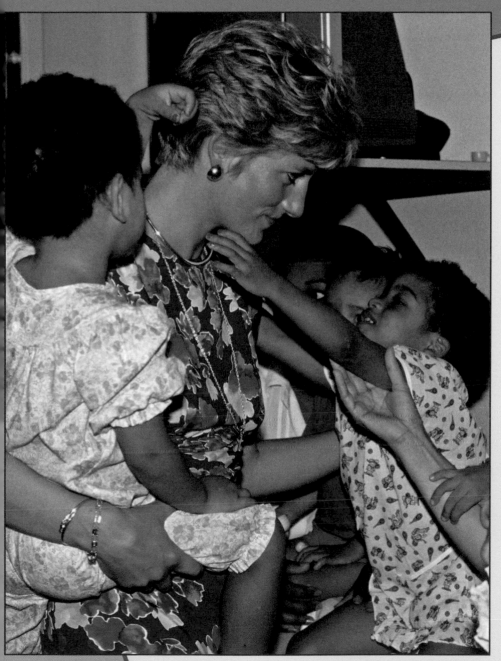

Princess Diana of Wales touched a different group of untouchables.

In 1987 not much was known about HIV infection. People knew it could develop into AIDS, a disease that damaged the immune system. They knew there was no cure.

But they didn't know exactly how it spread.

So getting close to someone with HIV or AIDS wasn't something many people were willing to do.

But then Great Britain's Princess Diana had her picture taken touching a person with HIV. As a beloved celebrity, she was in the perfect position to set an example. She shook hands, hugged, and held children and adults with HIV, showing the world there was nothing to fear.

"HIV DOES NOT MAKE PEOPLE DANGEROUS TO KNOW, SO YOU CAN SHAKE THEIR HANDS AND GIVE THEM A HUG. HEAVEN KNOWS THEY NEED IT."

Wear It Matters

Imagine a world where women have to wear long dresses and tight corsets. Imagine a world where women have to wear long hair whether they want to or not. Imagine a world where women of color never appear on a magazine cover.

Once upon a time, these were the rules. But these daring women dared to break them.

COCO CHANEL

Coco Chanel

AUGUST 19, 1883–JANUARY 10, 1971

FASHION DESIGNER

Chanel broke the rule that women wear women's clothes and men wear men's clothes. Instead of designing typical clothing for women in the early 1900s, Chanel created clothes inspired by menswear. Her clothes were loose-fitting and free from frills.

Zelda Fitzgerald

JULY 24, 1900–MARCH 10, 1948

FLAPPER

Fitzgerald broke the rule that girls should wear long hair and long skirts. Fitzgerald adopted a new style after World War I—and made it popular. She bobbed her hair and wore skimpy skirts to dance the night away.

Naomi Sims

MARCH 30, 1948–AUGUST 1, 2009

MODEL

Before Sims, black women weren't hired as cover models. Sims couldn't get a modeling agency to take her because of her skin color. So she hired her own photographers to jump start her career. In 1968 she was the first African-American model to grace the cover of *Ladies' Home Journal*.

PICTURE THIS

Dorothea Lange

MAY 26, 1895–OCTOBER 11, 1965

I didn't set out to change history. I just wanted to tell the real story of American citizens during the Great Depression in the 1920s and '30s. Unemployment was at an all-time high. People were jobless, poor, and desperate. I captured that experience as a photographer for the government. I took a lot of pictures of people who had been forced to move to find work or food. One picture I took, though, of a mother and her kids, really said it all. You can see the pain in the mother's eyes. It was always about telling that story, trying to get people to help.

Margaret Bourke-White

JUNE 14, 1904–AUGUST 27, 1971

I would do anything to get a good picture. I climbed around the top of New York City's Chrysler Building. I stood so close to pouring metal at a steel mill that I burned my face. My passion was telling stories with pictures.

I didn't think of myself as a rebel. I was just telling stories with my camera. But throughout my career, I was able to do a lot of firsts.

In 1930 I was the first western photographer allowed into the Soviet Union.

In 1935 I became the first female photographer at *Life* magazine.

During World War II, I became the first female war correspondent to travel with U.S. Army troops.

I was one of the first photographers in the German death camps too.

As I developed my talent, I wanted to use it to bring attention to social problems. In 1937 I took some shots of some African-Americans in Kentucky. They were standing in a breadline under a billboard showing a wealthy white family. That picture really showed how different life was in America for white families and African-Americans.

WORLD'S HIGHEST STANDARD OF LIVING

There's no way like the American Way

KATHARINE HEPBURN

MAY 12, 1907–JUNE 29, 2003

Katharine Hepburn was a beautiful, popular film actress in the 1930s. But even her fans got fed up when she refused to behave the way they thought a woman should. What did she do that was so horribly wrong? Well, for one thing fans said she wasn't grateful enough. Hepburn didn't like giving autographs and interviews like other starlets. They said her style was all wrong too. She went around town without make-up. And she preferred wearing pants rather than skirts or dresses.

Hepburn's eccentric attitude sometimes hurt her career. But she didn't cave in to cater to fans. And she set the attitude Hollywood still wears today. Stars act how they like and wear what they want. As Hepburn once said, *"If you obey all the rules, you miss all the fun."*

FLASHY, FLIRTY, AND FIT

THESE HIGH-PROFILE WOMEN MADE UNCONVENTIONAL
CHOICES FOR THE WHOLE WORLD TO SEE.

Mae West (August 17, 1893–November 22, 1980) was a playwright and actress who shocked audiences with her witty one-liners. She enjoyed using language to convey two meanings. While one meaning was usually innocent, the other was racy and scandalous. Long before it was acceptable for a woman to express her outrageous side, West started a tradition that continues today.

Jean Harlow (March 3, 1911–June 7, 1937) was known as a blond bombshell in movies of the early 1900s. But that's not all she was. Harlow brought a sense of humor to her roles, proving pretty women can be funny too.

Marilyn Monroe (June 1, 1926–August 5, 1962) created a beautiful image that made her famous. But today people remember her as much more than that. She's respected as a real woman who was powerful, vulnerable, innocent, and bold all at once.

Coloring The World

1929

I am captivated by the colorful landscape here in New Mexico. The skies are wide. The desert is barren. I've discovered the bones of an animal, bleached white by the sun. They seem beautiful and alive. I want to return here each summer and paint everything I see.

—Georgia

Georgia O'Keeffe

NOVEMBER 15, 1887–MARCH 6, 1986

Georgia O'Keeffe and Frida Kahlo didn't care what the world wanted to see. They were bold female painters of the early 20th century. They had unique visions. And together, they took art in a new direction.

1925

Since my accident on the bus, I have been bedridden for months.

I spend much of my time alone. But I have an easel and paints to keep me occupied. I paint the person I know best—myself.

—Frida

Frida Kahlo

JULY 6, 1907– JULY 13, 1954

ELLEN DEGENERES

JANUARY 26, 1958–

By April 1997 Ellen DeGeneres was already an accomplished comedienne and star of her own TV sitcom. But she was worried. Was her loyal audience about to stop laughing?

DeGeneres' show *Ellen* had been a popular show since 1994. The program was about Ellen Morgan, a character loosely based on herself. In 1997 DeGeneres made the decision that Morgan would tell the world she was a lesbian on the show. That meant the world would know DeGeneres was a lesbian too.

DeGeneres worried the news would turn her audience against her. She feared she'd lose everything she'd worked for. And when the episode aired, her worst fears came true. She was called "Ellen Degenerate" in the media. Major advertisers stopped supporting the show. Ratings dropped. A year later, the show was cancelled.

DeGeneres spent several years rebuilding her career. But she never regretted her decision to come out as gay. In interviews she said she did it for all the confused teenagers who needed her as a role model. She became a rebel for her cause and a pioneer for gay and lesbian rights.

The Write Way

Words can be powerful motivators. These female writers used the power of the pen to spread their messages of change.

Harriet Beecher Stowe

JUNE 14, 1811–JULY 1, 1896

When a new, harsher Fugitive Slave Law passed in 1850, Harriet Beecher Stowe was furious. She couldn't believe the law was demanding that all citizens help catch runaway slaves. She responded by writing a story for an anti-slavery newspaper. *Uncle Tom's Cabin* was an emotional story about the impact of slavery. Based on research and true stories, it was incredibly popular and stirred many to action against slavery. Stowe met President Abraham Lincoln during the U.S. Civil War, a war fought mostly over slavery. Legend has it that Lincoln said to her, "So you are the little woman who wrote the book that started this great war."

Nellie Bly

MAY 5, 1864–JANUARY 27, 1922

Nellie Bly was supposed to write stories about flower shows and fashions. But she wasn't going to miss a chance to use her job as a newspaper reporter for good. Bly let readers know how working girls suffered. She wrote about reforming divorce laws and the poor treatment of female prisoners. She even went undercover, in one case posing as a mentally ill person to enter an institution. Her colorful and honest articles exposed social problems and led to change.

Ida B. Wells

JULY 16, 1862–MARCH 25, 1931

Six months after Ida Wells was born, the Emancipation Proclamation set her family free. They had been slaves in the southern United States. And Wells would have been too if not for the new law.

But freedom from slavery didn't mean freedom from racism, prejudice, and violence. In 1884 Wells' life changed on a train. She had purchased a first-class ticket. But the train crew told her she had to move to the car for African-Americans. Wells refused. She was taken off the train, but she was set on the track toward racial justice.

Wells picked up a pen and began to write about the problem of violence against blacks. She went on to travel and speak publicly. She wanted the government to help keep African-Americans safe. Not everyone agreed with her ideas. She even received threats that forced her to leave the South. Still, she continued to write and work for justice.

Helen Keller

JUNE 27, 1880–JUNE 1, 1968

Helen Keller could not see even the brightest sunshine. She could not hear even the loudest thunder. No one expected much from this blind, deaf girl. What could a girl with her disabilities do?

ANYTHING SHE WANTED.

With the help of her teacher, Anne Sullivan, Keller learned

TOUCH-LIP READING

BRAILLE

TYPING

FINGER-SPELLING

She learned history, math, and science.

SHE LEARNED HOW TO SPEAK.

And then she started teaching. As an adult, Keller lectured all over the world, educating the public about blindness and deafness. She raised money for the American Foundation for the Blind. She lobbied the government for more financial assistance for blind people. Her work protected the rights of people with disabilities.

AND SHE SPENT HER LIFE PROVING JUST HOW CAPABLE AND INFLUENTIAL SHE COULD BE.

They are laughed at and called names. They are arrested, threatened, and even physically harmed. But even in tough situations, rebels don't back down. They stir controversy, inspire new ideas, and stand for what they believe in.

Women who rebel don't always set out to change the world. But their personal choices have an influence that can't be denied. By choosing their own way, despite risks and obstacles, these rebels pass on a message of empowerment to all.

1830s
Mary Somerville

1840s
Caroline Herschel
Elizabeth Cady Stanton
Harriet Tubman
Lucretia Mott

1850s
Harriet Beecher Stowe
Susan B. Anthony

1940s
Jacqueline Cochran
Mother Teresa
Nancy Harkness Love

1950s
Claudette Colvin
Marilyn Monroe
Rosa Parks

1960s
Betty Goldstein Friedan
Coretta Scott King
Naomi Sims

1970s
Barbara Walters
Gilda Radner
Gloria Steinem
Jane Curtin
Laraine Newman
Maya Angelou

1980s
Lois Jenson
Princess Diana
Sally Ride
Temple Grandin

1990s
Ai-jen Poo
Eileen Collins
Ellen DeGeneres
Erin Brockovich
Julia Butterfly Hill
Tina Fey

1860s
Lucy Stone

1880s
Helen Keller
Nellie Bly

1890s
Ida B. Wells

1900s
Marie Curie
Mother Jones

1910s
Alice Paul
Coco Chanel
Lucy Burns
Molly Brown

1920s
Bessie Coleman
Frida Kahlo
Georgia O'Keeffe
Jean Harlow
Zelda Fitzgerald

1930s
Amelia Earhart
Dorothea Lange
Katharine Hepburn
Mae West
Margaret Bourke-White

2000s
Amy Poehler
Cami Anderson
Comfort Freeman
Ellen Johnson Sirleaf
Leymah Gbowee
Razia Jan
Shirin Ebadi

2010s
Asmaa Mahfouz
Malala Yousafzai
Maryam Durani
Sadaf Rahimi
Tawakkol Karmen

INDEX

READ MORE

Ball, Heather. *Women Leaders Who Changed the World.* Great Women of Achievement. New York: Rosen Central, 2012.

McCann, Michelle Roehm and Amelie Welden. *Girls Who Rocked the World: Heroines from Joan of Arc to Mother Teresa.* New York: Aladdin, 2012.

Tougas, Shelley. *Girls Rule!: Amazing Tales of Female Leaders.* Girls Rock! North Mankato, Minn.: Capstone Press, 2014.

INTERNET SITES

FactHound offers a safe, fun way to find Internet sites related to this book. All of the sites on FactHound have been researched by our staff.

Here's all you do:

Visit *www.facthound.com*

Type in this code: 9781476502328